Amazing Gospel Magic: Bible Lessons With A Magical Appeal

www.mymagicrabbit.com

Magic Marketing Co; The Pickle Group, LLC
Freeport, Ohio 43973

Dr. Dennis C. Regling
Piedmont Christian Ministries
P.O.Box 118; Piedmont, Ohio 43983
Telephone: (800) 858-5402 www.WinTheChildren.com
Email. dregling@gmail.com

More Gospel Magic at www.mymagicrabbit.com

"The grass withereth, the flower fadeth: but the word of our God shall stand for ever."
Isaiah 40:8

The Author
"Mr. Dennis"
Dennis Regling

Children are without a doubt the world's most fruitful mission field. They are the most responsive to the gospel today because they are searching for love, acceptance, security and forgiveness. The Lord Jesus Christ provides all of these.

Children for the most part are not hardened from indulgence in deep sin. These youngsters are open, tender, trusting, receptive and are usually willing to admit their sin, accept Christ's forgiveness and trust in His Word. But like everyone else, "They will not seek, they must be sought. They will not come, they must be brought. They will not learn, they must be taught."

Our burden is to help equip the local church in children's ministry so that the greatest number of souls can be saved in these last days.

Many prominent Christians were saved as children. Matthew Henry was saved at age ten; Isaac Watts at age nine; Jonathan Edwards at age seven; the list goes on and on.The good seed of God's Word can be planted into children's minds and hearts so that an abundant harvest will be reaped.

The Christian churches lose more children of Christian parents, than they gain new converts by means of evangelistic efforts.

It is important to reach adults with the Gospel. Godly parents raise Godly children. Unfortunately, not all parents are Godly.
For the last 15 years I have preached in juvenile detention centers, county jails and state prisons. As God opens the doors, I will continue to do so, but I would rather get the children and the teens before they get arrested.

God has burdened my heart for the young people today. My wife and I love nothing more than sharing God's Word and God's love with children and teens. We have ministered at Vacation Bible School programs, Family Crusades, Bible Camps and Special Events.

Dr. Dennis C. Regling
Piedmont Christian Ministries
www.WinTheChildren.com

Why Use Gospel Illusions or Gospel Magic Object Lessons

Creating the anticipation that something special is about to happen gives a big boost to children's interest in your lesson! Increased interest is just one of the benefits of using illusions in your classroom.

Gospel illusions, simply object lessons with a special effect, are also helpful because they do well at illustrating abstract concepts such as salvation or the Trinity.

THE TRUTH THAT GOD IS POWERFUL!

What you need:
3 plates/dishes
3 paper towels
1 bowl of water
3 pieces of paper
1 lighter/match
3 glass jars or glasses
3 pens or pencils

The trick: Completely wet one paper towel and press it flat down on the plate. Light the piece of paper and let it begin to burn. Place the paper inside the glass and immediately turn it over onto the paper towel. Let the flame burn out, then lift up the glass. The glass will adhere to the paper towel and plate.

Script:
Our Bible verse today says: "Therefore, my beloved brethren, be ye stedfast, unmoveable, always abounding in the work of the Lord, forasmuch as ye know that your labour is not in vain in the Lord." 1 Corinthians 15:58

There are so many wonderful things that we can do for God. We can pray that our friends and family members will come to know Him. We can help people out by giving them things that they might need like food or clothing or money. What are some other things we can do for God? (Wait for responses.)

Yes. Those are all great ideas of things we can do for God. And our Bible verse says that ANYTHING we do for God will NEVER be wasted. There is another Bible verse that says "when we are weak, God is strong." 2 Corinthians 12:10

So, even if we can only do little things for the Lord, God will still show Himself powerful to all who can see. I have here a plate, a paper towel, and a glass. Let's let the plate remind you of you. Now let's let this paper

9

towel remind us of Jesus whom the Bible calls "the Living Water". (Immerse paper towel in the water.)
I think this name of Jesus reminds us of a water fountain that just keeps giving water and never stops. God gave you His one and only Son, Jesus. (Flatten the paper towel onto the plate.)

Here is a a pretty glass. This glass will remind us of the good work we can do for God.

Here are 3 pieces of paper. (Hold up the piece of paper.) Can I have 3 of you each write an example of a good deed that can be done for God? (Wait for response and write it down on the piece of paper.) Excellent! I will write that good deed on this paper.

Here is a lighter. I am going to light this piece of paper, because another Bible verse says, "Let your light shine before men so they may see your good deeds and praise the Father in Heaven." (Matthew 5:16)

I am now going to put the good deed in the pretty deed holder.
I am going to turn this work for God over onto the plate, because I want to give to God all that I do for Him.

The light is burning out, but don't worry, God is still at work. He has taken the good deed that you or I did and can show the world around us that He is strong and powerful!

Now, what will happen if we don't give our good deeds over to the Lord? Instead our good works are just all about us. (Take a second plate and place the wet paper towel on it. Light a second piece of paper and place it in a second glass, but don't turn it over and try and lift the plate. Of course, it won't work.)

Hmm. A Good work plus No connection to God and His Son Jesus equals no power. You see, when we don't do our good deeds for the Lord, God's power won't be able to shine through us.

But if we give our good works to the Lord (Do the whole trick with the 3rd plate and so on...) then God's power will be seen by those around us and nothing we do for Him will ever be wasted.

10

Loop the Loop

Effect:

Three paper loops are displayed. Each one is cut lengthwise with a pair of scissors. The first turns into two separate loops as expected, but the second produces two loops linked together and the third produces one large loop.

Method:

When you make the first loop simply bring the two ends straight together and fasten with glue or tape. For the second loop, give the paper a full twist before fastening the ends together, and with the last one make a half twist. If the loops are fairly long the twists will not be noticed. If you use crepe paper streamers the nature of the paper also helps to hide the twists.

Be sure that you know which loop is which, and that you stay away from the edges when cutting. The twists in the paper do all the work, but your presentation is what will create the "magic".

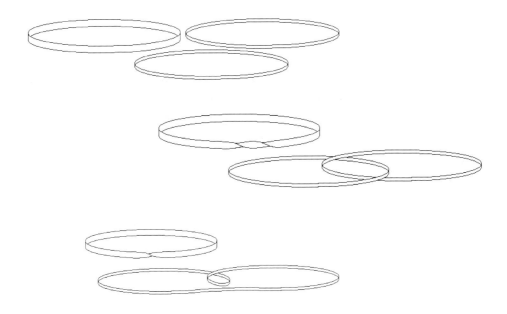

Presentation:
I use this effect to illustrate being made complete in Christ. When God first made Adam and Eve they were at one with Him, having daily fellowship in the garden, but when they chose to disobey (Cut the first band) their sin separated them from God.

Some people try to get back into fellowship with God through doing good works, going to church or other things in order to make up for their own wrongdoings.

(Cut the second strip, with the full twist.) They fail to realize that only Christ's sacrifice on the cross can atone for our sins. They may be connected to the Christian movement, but they are still not complete in Christ. Only by accepting Christ as Lord and Savior

(Cut third loop) can we find complete forgiveness and eternal life. Through His work, not our own, we can be one with Him. (Display large single loop.)

Which Way - A Gospel Optical Illusion

Romans 3:23 *For all have sinned, and come short of the glory of God;*

Effect: An arrow that is clearly pointing one way is seen to instantly, and visibly change direction.

Props: A sign depicting HEAVEN, a sign depicting HELL, a picture of a large arrow, a clear water glass, pitcher of water.

Note: The glass should be made of glass, and not plastic.

Performance: As Christians, we believe that there is an ultimate goal, or direction for our lives. It is an eternity spent in Heaven, with our Lord. However, as you will see by looking at our display, there is a built-in problem with our being able to reach that goal. You see, we all have sin in our lives (Rom 3:23), and that sin prevents us from heading in a direction toward Heaven, and actually steers us toward Hell!

Let me demonstrate what happens to a person's life, the moment he or she believes on Jesus for the forgiveness of sin.

Place the glass in front of the arrow, and you can still clearly see that the arrow points toward the sign marked HELL.

Our lives are to be as vessels, willing and able to hold whatever we put into them. Looking at our example, it would appear that no matter how "clean and clear" our lives appear to be, without the Lord Jesus, we are not only empty inside, but we are headed for an eternity in Hell, apart from Christ.

Let's suggest, just for a moment, however, that the water in this glass (hold up glass of water) represents the Word of God. We know from John 1:1 "In the beginning was the Word, and the Word was with God, and the Word was God."

In other words, when we refer to the Word, we are also referencing Jesus Christ Himself.

And let's take a look at what happens when we allow the Word, (or Jesus) to come into our lives by believing on Him to forgive our sins, and change our eternal destination.

(Pour the glass of water into the first glass and watch as before your very eyes, the direction of the arrow appears to change, to point toward HEAVEN!

What this little illusion is showing us is a truth that can change our very lives for an eternity! If we would only believe on the Lord to forgive us of our sins, He is faithful and just to do just that!

And the change in our eternal destination is an instant thing! When Christ is in us, and we are in Him, we are on our way to Heaven. and that is a truth worth shouting about!

Additional Note: This little illusion is an illusion for the eyes, but it is also a scientific principle in action - that of "refraction". Refraction is what happens when light is "bent" through a lens of some sort. and just such a lens is created when we add the water to the clear glass. Have fun with this not only can you show the audience a nifty little science lesson, but you can share the truth that is capable of changing their lives for an eternity!

Ticket to Heaven

I use a story about two friends Mike and Joe who live in a house (see # 5 in illustration)

Talk about how they planned on going on a vacation. So they got on a airplane (then I fold the house in half and make it look like an airplane and fly it around a bit Then I crash it into one of the kids.) Then they died.

Mike and Joe are now waiting in line to get to heaven. Mike has a ticket(fold wings down flat so it looks like #6 in illustration). Joe doesn't.

Joe starts asking how Mike got a ticket? Mike explains to him when he was a child he Gave his life to God and lived for him. Joe was scared because he never thought God was real. Joe thought the Ticket was what was going to get him into heaven So he started fighting with Mike trying to get the ticket.

In the process Joe tore 2 pieces off the ticket. He thought since he has most of the ticket he should be good now. (Keep the hell pieces to use next and give the cross piece to a volunteer and tell them to hold that piece and don't open it till the end.)

God comes out during judgment and asks Joe why he believes he should go to heaven. Joe gives God his ticket and says because I have this ticket. (start unfolding the papers and start spelling out hell)

God takes the ticket and tells Joe that the ticket is not what saves you. Since you never had a relationship with me and never believed and gave your life to me. This is where you will be for eternity. (By now you should have hell already spelled out) Now Mike is really nervous because he saw his friend just get sent to hell.

God asks Mike why should I let you into heaven. Read Romans 6:23 and Romans10:9-10. (Take Hell papers and start to make it say life) Mike was speechless. God said since you gave your life to me as a child and lived for me. This is your destination (have volunteer unfold cross paper) since my son paid the price for your sins.

15

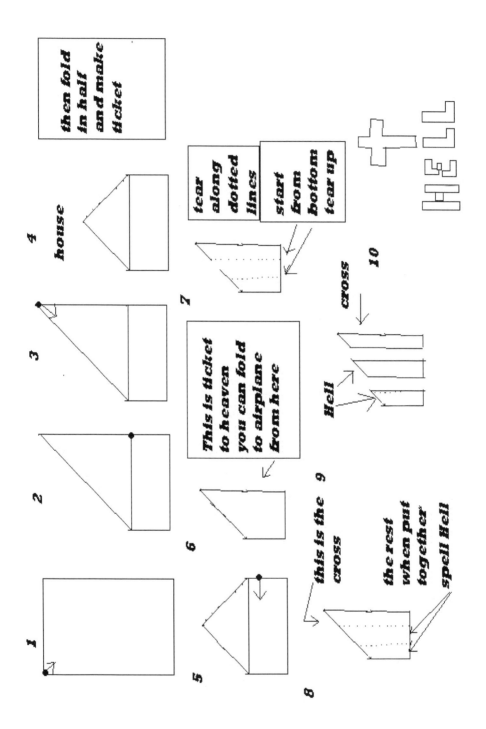

1

2

3

house 4

5

6

This is ticket to heaven you can fold to airplane from here 7

then fold in half and make ticket

tear along dotted lines

start from bottom tear up

8 *the rest when put together spell Hell*

this is the cross 9

Hell

cross 10

HELL

ALL FROM FROM AN EMPTY BOX

You can make lots of stuff appear from a small cereal box or snack cracker box.

From an empty cereal box, you produce some silk handkerchiefs or other objects.

Remove the top of a cereal box. Cut a neat hole in the back of the box. With some light cardboard, make a triangular box (Fig.1). Attach the secret box over the hole in the cereal box with tape or glue (Fig. 2). The secret box hinges into the box or out of it.

Place the items you are going to produce in the secret compartment of the box.

To do the trick, show the cereal box empty box holding your hand over the secret compartment as shown. Of course, you never show the back of the box!

Turn the box upright and reach into the top of the box, then into the secret compartment to produce the items you previously placed there.

Message: Philippians 4:19 *"But my God shall supply all your need according to his riches in glory by Christ Jesus."*

I talk about how we all have wants and needs, but our focus should be on our heavenly Father who has promised to supply all our needs.

Notice also the limits of supply: all your needs. It doesn't say, all your wants. Our wants are sometimes far beyond our needs.

Dr. H.A. Ironside used to say he delighted to walk through Woolworth's dime stores because it was always such a comfort to him to see so many things he could get along without.

There are so many wants in our lives, and really so relatively few needs. God has promised to supply your needs, and you must let him decide what your needs are.

Notice finally the method of supply. It's according to his riches in glory in Christ Jesus. There are many kinds of riches. There are the riches of his goodness which are available to all people. He makes the sun shine and the rain to fall upon the just and the unjust. Then there are the riches of his grace which are available only to sinners who admit their need. God's grace takes over and forgives and cleanses and gives us purity and all we need.

Then there is the riches of his glory in Christ Jesus. This is available for saints, to those who know him. All that he has in terms of the glory and fullness of his deity is available to any believer. The weakest saint holds in his hands all that the greatest saint ever had. He has Christ, and in having Christ he has everything!

I show the empty box. Then I talk about the things we need and Christ's supply and start producing items from the box.

I'll produce small plastic food items, a picture of a house. Some coins or bills. (I like to use the expanding production bills available in magic shops.) And other items.

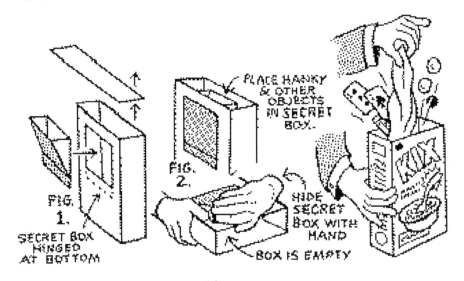

MULTIPLYING COINS

I like to use this trick to illustrate the account of the multiplying loaves and fishes. I also use it in another lesson to talk about evangelism and how we can spread the gospel of Jesus Christ.

Effect:
You count out four coins, placing them on a table. You gather up the coins, then place them on the table again. You now have five coins!
Before you begin, secretly attach a coin to the underside of the table with a bit of soap or wax.

Method:
Show the other four coins, counting them at the edge of the table. Be sure that everybody sees that your hands are empty.

Use one hand to scoop the visible the coins into your other hand, which goes below the edge of the table to catch the coins. At the same time, use the hand below the table to release the hidden coin. Immediately make a fist around the coins.

After saying a few magic words or tapping your wand with a magic wand (or a pencil or pen), open your hand to show that you now have five coins!

RELEASE
HIDDEN
COIN

MORE MULTIPLYING MONEY
CHRISTIAN REWARDS! A "HUNDREDFOLD!"

Magic with money is a real crowd-pleaser.

Four coins become eight.
Before you start the trick, place four coins in the spine of a book. When the book is closed, the coins will not come out. Now open the book and place four coins in the book. As you slide the coins into your hand, the other four will join them.

Close your hand. Make a magical gesture, then show that the four coins have become eight!

MARK 10:28-31 CHRISTIAN REWARDS! A "HUNDREDFOLD!"

In this Text Jesus discusses the matter of Rewards! In fact, "hundredfold" rewards!

"Then Peter began to say unto him, Lo, we have left all, and have followed thee. And Jesus answered and said, Verily I say unto you, There is no man that hath left house, or brethren, or sisters, or father, or mother, or wife, or children, or lands, for my sake, and the gospel's, but he shall receive an hundredfold now in this time, houses, and brethren, and sisters, and mothers, and children, and lands, with persecutions; and in the world to come eternal life. But many that are first shall be last; and the last first."

DOT'S SOME TRICK

Effect: You show a card with one spot on one side and four on the other and three on the other side and six on the other and one one the other.

Make a card with two spots on one side and five spots on the other, as shown in the illustration.

The domino trick.

As you hold the card initially, one hand hides the dots on the end of the side with two spots, making it look like there is only one spot. Take the card in your other hand, by the side, hiding the middle spot on the side with five sides. Turn your hand over. It looks like there are four spots.

Take the card in your other hand, hiding the empty space above the two spots. Turn your hand over, it looks like three spots. Take the card by the side, hiding the empty space on the other side, it looks like six spots!

Application:
Galatians 6:7 B*e not deceived; God is not mocked: for whatsoever a man soweth, that shall he also reap.*

I use this to discuss how easy we can be deceived. We assume the dots are six and three and one because we see these patterns every day on dice, dominoes and playing cards.

Similarly, Satan can deceive us by making things appear to be good, even when they are bad for us.

The account of Adam and Eve is also a great illustration of Satan's deceptive practices.

TORN & RESTORED PAPER

Effect:

You tear a sheet of tissue paper (or a piece from a napkin) into several pieces, roll the pieces into a ball, say the magic words, then unroll the ball to show that the paper is whole again.

How to apparently tear up a napkin, then restore it.

Before you begin the trick, take a duplicate piece of paper and roll it into a ball.

Hide the duplicate ball of paper in your hand as your tear up (or tear down) the other piece of paper. Roll the torn-up pieces in a ball then switch the two balls of paper. Hide the ball of torn-up pieces as you undo the other ball to show that the paper is restored.

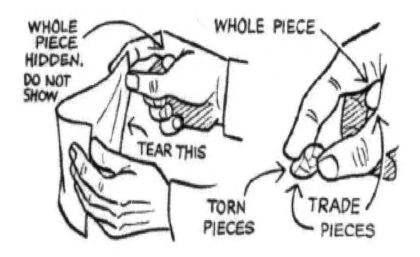

Application:

As a mighty warrior and the commander of the Syrian army, Naaman may have had scuffed skin and battle scars, but he also had a serious skin disease—leprosy. When a servant suggested that the prophet Elisha could heal him, Naaman visited him.

He followed Elisha's instructions, and his diseased flesh became "like the flesh of a little child" (2 Kings 5:14). This cure left Naaman better off both physically and spiritually. After being healed, he proclaimed, "Now I know that there is no God in all the earth, except in Israel" (v.15). Through this miraculous experience, he learned that there is only one true God (1 Cor. 8:6).

Like Naaman, we can learn important lessons about God as a result of our life experiences. Receiving a blessing may show us about His mercy and goodness (Matt. 7:11). Surviving or enduring a trial may help us see God's sufficiency and care. Growing in knowledge of Him (2 Peter 3:18) will always leave us better off spiritually than we were before.

By following God's instructions, he will restore us to fellowship with him. He forgives our sin and empowers us to serve.

Love Routine for the Pom Pom stick!

This routine uses a Pom-Pom Stick. This is a magician's prop available from magic dealers. (Google search Pom-Pom Pole Magic)

Begin with strings the same length! I appreciate that your colours might well be different to mine! It does not matter as they are of no real significance.

I have here a very unusual Gizmo! It's my 'Pom Pom' stick! It is an unusual item made up of several different yet interconnecting parts. As you can see on this side the Yellow 'Pom Pom' is connected to the Green 'Pom Pom' and the green 'Pom Pom' is connected to the Yellow 'Pom Pom'. On the other side the Red 'Pom Pom' is connected to the Black 'Pom Pom' and the Black 'Pom Pom' is connected to the Red 'Pom Pom'.

Nothing unusual there you say!

Strangely however the Green 'Pom Pom' is also connected to the Black 'Pom Pom' whilst at the same time being connected to the Yellow 'Pom Pom'. Weirder still the Yellow 'Pom Pom' is also connected to the Black 'Pom Pom' which interestingly all the time retains its link to the Red 'Pom Pom'. The Red 'Pom Pom' even more strangely remains connected to the Black 'Pom Pom' whilst also connected to the Green 'Pom Pom' and the Yellow 'Pom Pom'.

Altogether then an unusual mix of interrelated connections! All of which makes it ideal for me to try to explain the word Love!

We have a tendency in English to use the one word love to speak of a whole range of emotions and relationships. I love chocolate and I love my wife. I love football and I love dogs. I love reading but I also love jogging! The question is, "Do I love chocolate in the same way I love my wife or the dog for that matter"? Obviously there is a difference, well at least my wife hopes so!

Pom Poms now back where we started with even strings

In Greek, the language of the New Testament, there are many words used to express the word love! Let me highlight what for me are 4 of the most important.

Taking the Yellow PomPom:
The first word is 'Phileo' which is friendship love! The sort of love we have for a good friend!

Taking the Green PomPom:

The second is 'Storge' which is filial love. The kind of love you would have for your Mum or Dad, brother or sister!

Taking the Black PomPom:
The third is 'Eros' which is sensual love. We get our word erotic from here. It is the kind of love most featured in the media or on film. It can at best be something amazingly beautiful and at worst incredibly selfish and damaging. It can get you into trouble. Talk to Jon Terry, Tiger Woods, or any number of famous actors, sports people or politicians!

Taking the Red PomPom:
The fourth is 'Agape'! Agape is sacrificial love. Agape love costs. Agape love is more about what you want than what I want! We see Agape love modelled in Jesus the one who came to serve and not to be served. The one who surrendered His own life in order that we might have life!

Four words then! Phileo, Storge, Eros, Agape. Four words that all mean love but completely different aspects of that one word.

But what happens if we link Agape to Phileo? Taking the Red Pom Pom and linking it to the Yellow Pom Pom: We get a friend that sticks closer than a brother. A friend that works for your success even at the expense of their own! A friend that will not just be there for you but one that would even lay down their lives for you!

Then if we link Agape to Storge! Taking the Red Pom Pom and linking it to the Green Pom Pom: We then have family relationships that work on an amazingly deep level. Relationships that will weather the storms that life throws at us! Relationships that exist for one another!

25

Is it possible that we can link Agape with Eros? Taking the Red Pom Pom and linking it to the Black Pom Pom: Song of Solomon in the Bible legitimises erotic love in the context of committed loving relationships. Christian Marriage, where each partner's highest goal is to love and to cherish the one God has given them, is the right place for sexual relationships. Agape love provides the safe zone in which sexual love might be played out to each other's fullest pleasure!

Four words all incredibly interconnected! One last time showing the interlinking of all Pom Poms till they hang equal length strings with the Pom Poms suspended together over the bar:

Too good to be true you say! Where do we find Agape love? The Bible says that God is Love. Agape is the word the Bible uses to describe Christ's love for us. It is in relationship with God that we receive His love into our heart and lives. What is more wonderful is that all of this comes, as Agape love always comes, Gripping the strings either side of the bar pull apart! With no strings attached!

Routine is concluded with the bar apart as to rejoin it diminishes the impact of Agape Love!

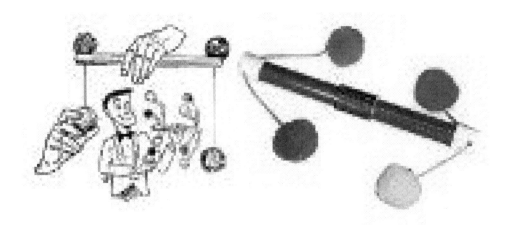

Escaping Sin Chain Escape

A simple chain escape trick ball chain loop routine

The following item is for a simple chain escape. It may be performed using a loop of string but it looks much better if a ball chain loop is used.

Routine

Loop the chain over the first and second fingers of the left hand so that the loop hangs down on the palm side of the left hand.

Hold the lower end of the chain with the right hand as shown in the diagram below.

With the left thumb, hook the length of chain that runs from the left second finger down to the right hand. This will give the loop at "A".

Without letting the chain slip from the thumb or fingers, lift the loop "A" with the right hand and pass the whole of the left hand through loop "A".

Place the left first and second fingers in your mouth and hold them with your teeth to stop the chain escaping (or so it seems).

By simply lifting the chain that is at your left wrist off over your thumb and take off the loop that is round your thumb the loop of chain will come free. The description may sound a bit difficult but give it a try and you will soon get the hang of it.

Alternative:

Instead of holding your fingers between your teeth a volunteer can hold your fingers to try and stop the chain escaping. If this method is used then the handling will have to be smoother to prevent exposure of the release.

Escaping The Chains Of Sin

The Bible teaches that with temptation, God always makes a way of escape... "There hath no temptation taken you but such as is common to man: but God is faithful, who will not suffer you to be tempted above that ye are able; but will with the temptation also make a way to escape, that ye may be able to bear it" (1st Corinthians 10:13). No one has an excuse to sin. We all experience the same types of temptations throughout life. The Bible teaches that we always have a choice, to do right or wrong.

Thankfully, there is help available from the Lord Jesus Himself, Who was also tempted. Hebrews 2:18, "For in that he himself hath suffered being tempted, he is able to succour them that are tempted." The Greek word for "succour" in Hebrews 2:18 is boetheo meaning "to aid or relieve." Literally, it means to help. Jesus fully understands the overwhelming power of temptation. If we submit ourselves unto God and resist the Devil as the Bible teaches in James 4:7, he will flee from us. Temptations will come and go; but Jesus Christ is "the same yesterday, and to day, and for ever" (Hebrews 13:8).

James 1:12-14 clearly states... *"Blessed is the man that endureth temptation: for when he is tried, he shall receive the crown of life, which the Lord hath promised to them that love him. Let no man say when he is tempted, I am tempted of God: for God cannot be tempted with evil, neither tempteth he any man: But every man is tempted, when he is drawn away of his own lust, and enticed."*

We learn three divine truths from this passage of Scripture:

- Our love for Jesus should cause us to want to live right, i.e., keep His commands.
- God never tempts anyone to do wrong.
- We sin because we want to by yielding to our own lusts.

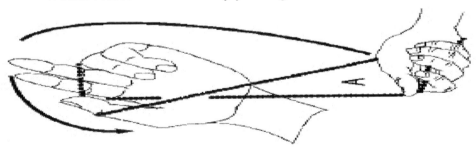

- Turn sideways to see how to hold rope.

Forcing Card

Color forcing card device for forcing a color, picture of other item.

There are often times when you would like to force a particular color, picture or other item. This novel device allows you to do just that. In fact you can force one color from a choice of six.

The device is simply an oblong card divided into six squares. Each square is a different color. The color that you wish to force is the shaded square in the diagram.

How to use the device

Get a spectator to choose any number from one to six inclusive. When they tell you their number you pick up the card in the position that will enable you to count to your force color. Please note that the squares do not have numbers printed on them, hey are simply there in the diagram to show you how to count for the number chosen.

Once you arrive at your force color you can then proceed with any effect that needs this color to be selected.

With this you may simply force a color. I prefer to have six cards. Each will have one of the colors from the card on one side and a picture on the other.

Have the volunteer pick a number or roll a die. You then count to your force color on the chart. Pick up the matching card and reveal the picture.

A great way to use this is to have five "works" on five of the cards. Maybe, giving, attending church, baptism, etc. With appropriate pictures. The sixth card, the card of the force color, will have a cross on it, and perhaps a Bible verse.

I ask the volunteer to pick a number and we will see the way to Heaven. After showing the 5 wrong cards, I reveal the chosen color has the cross.

I ask the volunteer to pick a number and we will see the way to Heaven.
After showing the 5 wrong cards, I reveal the chosen color has the cross.
The only way to Heaven.

You can use this same device any time you want to force one item out of
six.

1	2	3
4	5	6

1	2
3	4
5	6

1	4
2	5
3	6

1	4
2	5
3	6

1	2
3	4
5	6

1	2	3
4	5	6

The Jumping Rings

Effect: The magician holds a rope between his hands. There are three knots tied on it, and on the center knot is tied to a wire hanger. The magician says a magic word and FLASH, right before everyone's eyes, the hanger jumps from the center knot to the right knot!

How to: Use a strong piece of rope, about 3' long. It should be about ¼" thick. Take a look at the drawing below these instructions. It shows 4 knots on the rope. Knots B, C and D are regular knots. The hanger is tied to knot C. But knot A isn't a regular knot, it is a "slip knot." It looks pretty much like the others, but when pulled by the ends of the rope, comes undone.

What to do:
Begin the trick with knot D covered by your right hand. Hold the rope so that knots A, B, and C are showing.

Say: "Here we have three knots. Notice that a hanger is tied onto the end knot. But watch … Abracadabra!"

Now, do two things:

First: Pull the rope very tight between your hands. This will cause the slip-knot (A) to come undone. It seems to disappear.

Second: Pull the rope again with the left hand. Slide knot D from your right hand. When you do this fast, it looks to the audience as if the hanger has jumped from the end knot to the center knot.

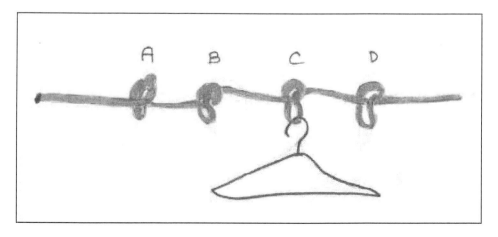

Application:

I use this illusion to illustrate that we are to be "in Christ," not just beside Christ. Christianity is life changing.

Ephesians 2:10 - *For we are his workmanship, created **in Christ Jesus** unto good works, which God hath before ordained that we should walk in them.*

It is important to see how we become "in Christ." Paul says, "You did not receive a spirit that makes you a slave again to fear." When the Spirit of God came into your heart, he did not make you a slave to fear.

Remember how Paul puts that again in Second Timothy 1:7: "You have not received a spirit of fear, but of power and of love and of a sound mind," (2 Timothy 1:7 KJV).

That is the nature of the Holy Spirit. What did the Spirit do? Paul says, "You received the Spirit who makes you sons," or, literally, "the Spirit of adoption, who adopted you as sons." How did you become a son of God? Well, the Spirit of God found you, and found me, and he adopted us into God's family.

Four Steps To Jesus

This chart can be made as big or small as you like. It is an excellent witnessing tool, as well as a fun class activity.

Use the chart on the book cover or make your own.

START BY CHOOSING A BLUE SQUARE THAT BEST REPRE-SENTS WHAT YOU LIKE TO DO FOR FUN.
(THEN FOLLOW 4 STEPS)
1. Move LEFT or RIGHT to the nearest YELLOW square
2. Move UP or DOWN to the nearest BLUE square
3. Move DIAGONALLY to the nearest YELLOW square
4. Move LEFT or RIGHT to the nearest BLUE square

HERE IS THE 4 STEPS TO COME TO GOD
1. Admit you have sinned (Romans 3:23)
2. Know we are accountable for sin and deserve to go to Hell (Romans 6:23)
3. Believe and trust what Jesus did on the cross for your sins (John 3:16 or Romans 5:8)
9) - doing good stuff won't get us there (Ephesians 2:8)
10) - 4. Surrender your life Christ and give God ownership by confessing and believing (Romans 10:9
: (remember salvation is not by saying words, it's a heart thing, putting your faith and trust in God)

Playing Sports	Reading God's Word	Hang with Family or Friends	Shopping
Peace in Life	Showing Love to Others	Praying	Jesus Christ and the Cross
Playing Videogames	Eating Favorite Food	Going to Church	Being Out-doors

How to use it

The square trick is neat in that it helps you start a conversation and keep one going jumping from a secular topic to a religious topic and eventually leads you to talk about Jesus and what he did on the cross. The neat thing about this trick is no matter what choice the individual makes (as long as they follow the instructions exactly). The person you are talking to will end up on Jesus Christ and the Cross by the time you get to the last step.

To schedule Dennis Regling to preach and teach at your church or event, email: dregling@gmail.com or go to www.WinTheChildren.com

Be sure to search Amazon for Dennis' other gospel magic and Christian books.

36645079R00023

Made in the USA
Charleston, SC
09 December 2014